SAS Publishing

MW00906196

SAS/OR® 9.1 User's Guide:
Constraint Programming

The Power to Know.

The correct bibliographic citation for this manual is as follows: SAS Institute Inc. 2004. *SAS/OR® 9.1 User's Guide: Constraint Programming*. Cary, NC: SAS Institute Inc.

SAS/OR® 9.1 User's Guide: Constraint Programming

Contents

Credits

Documentation

Writing	Gehan A. Corea
Editing	Virginia Clark
Documentation Support	Tim Arnold, Michelle Opp
Technical Review	Edward P. Hughes, Radhika V. Kulkarni, Rob Pratt

Software

PROC CLP	Gehan A. Corea

Support Groups

Software Testing	Rob Pratt
Technical Support	Tonya Chapman

What's New in SAS/OR 9 and 9.1

Overview

SAS/OR software contains several new and enhanced features since SAS 8.2. Brief descriptions of the new features appear in the following sections. For more information, refer to the SAS/OR documentation, which is now available in the following six volumes:

- SAS/OR User's Guide: Bills of Material Processing
- SAS/OR User's Guide: Constraint Programming
- SAS/OR User's Guide: Local Search Optimization
- SAS/OR User's Guide: Mathematical Programming
- SAS/OR User's Guide: Project Management
- SAS/OR User's Guide: The QSIM Application

The online help can also be found under the corresponding classification.

The BOM Procedure

The BOM procedure in *SAS/OR User's Guide: Bills of Material Processing* was introduced in Version 8.2 of the SAS System to perform bill of material processing. Several new features have been added to the procedure, enabling it to read all product structure records from a product structure data file and all part "master" records from a part master file, and compose the combined information into indented bills of material. This data structure mirrors the most common method for storing bill-of-material data in enterprise settings; the part master file contains data on each part while the product structure file holds data describing the various part-component relationships represented in bills of material.

The PMDATA= option on the PROC BOM statement enables you to specify the name of the Part Master data set. If you do not specify this option, PROC BOM uses the Product Structure data set (as specified in the DATA= option) as the Part Master data set. The BOM procedure now looks up the Part, LeadTime, Requirement, QtyOnHand, and ID variables in the Part Master data set. On the other hand, the Component and Quantity variables remain in the Product Structure data set.

You can use the NRELATIONSHIPS= (or NRELTS=) option to specify the number of parent-component relationships in the Product Structure data set. You have greater control over the handling of redundant relationships in the Product Structure data set using the DUPLICATE= option.

Several options have been added to the STRUCTURE statement enabling you to specify information related to the parent-component relationships. In particular, the variable specified with the PARENT= option identifies the parent item, while the variables listed in the LTOFFSET= option specify lead-time offset information. You can also specify variables identifying scrap factor information for all parent-component relationships using the SFACTOR= option. The RID= option identifies all variables in the Product Structure data set that are to be included in the Indented BOM output data set.

The CLP Procedure (Experimental)

9.1

The new CLP procedure in *SAS/OR User's Guide: Constraint Programming* is an experimental finite domain constraint programming solver for solving constraint satisfaction problems (CSPs) with linear, logical, global, and scheduling constraints. In addition to having an expressive syntax for representing CSPs, the solver features powerful built-in consistency routines and constraint propagation algorithms, a choice of nondeterministic search strategies, and controls for guiding the search mechanism that enable you to solve a diverse array of combinatorial problems.

The CPM Procedure

The CPM procedure in *SAS/OR User's Guide: Project Management* adds more options for describing resource consumption by activities, enhancing its applicability to production scheduling models.

A new keyword, RESUSAGE, has been added to the list of values for the OBSTYPE variable in the Resource data set. This keyword enables you to specify whether a resource is consumed at the beginning or at the end of a given activity.

The MILESTONERESOURCE option enables you to specify a nonzero usage of consumable resources for milestone activities. For example, this option is useful if you wish to designate specific milestones to be the points of payment for a subcontractor. The MILESTONENORESOURCE option is the current default behavior of the CPM procedure, which indicates that all resource requirements are to be ignored for milestone activities.

The GA Procedure (Experimental)

9.1

The new GA procedure in *SAS/OR User's Guide: Local Search Optimization* facilitates the application of genetic algorithms to general optimization. Genetic algorithms adapt the biological processes of natural selection and evolution to search for optimal solutions. The procedure can be applied to optimize problems involving integer, continuous, binary, or combinatorial variables. The GA procedure is especially useful for finding optima for problems where the objective function may have discontinuities or may not otherwise be suitable for optimization by traditional calculus-based methods.

The GANTT Procedure

The GANTT procedure in *SAS/OR User's Guide: Project Management* includes a new option for controlling the width of the Gantt chart. The CHARTWIDTH= option specifies the width of the axis area as a percentage of the total Gantt chart width. This option enables you to generate Gantt charts that are consistent in appearance, independent of the total time spanned by the project.

The LP Procedure

The performances of primal and dual simplex algorithms in the LP procedure (*SAS/OR User's Guide: Mathematical Programming*) have been significantly improved on large scale linear or mixed integer programming problems.

The PM Procedure

The new options added to the CPM procedure are also available with PROC PM.

The QP Procedure (Experimental)

The new QP procedure in *SAS/OR User's Guide: Mathematical Programming* implements a primal-dual predictor-corrector interior-point algorithm for large sparse quadratic programs. Depending on the distribution of the eigenvalues of the Hessian matrix, H, two main classes of quadratic programs are distinguished (assuming minimization):

9.1

- convex: H is positive semi-definite
- nonconvex: H has at least one negative eigenvalue

Diagonal and nonseparable Hessian matrices are recognized and handled automatically.

Bill of Material Post Processing Macros

Several macros enable users to generate miscellaneous reports using the Indented BOM output data set from the BOM procedure in *SAS/OR User's Guide: Bills of Material Processing*. Other transactional macros perform specialized transactions for maintaining and updating the bills of material for a product, product line, plant, or company.

Chapter 1
The CLP Procedure (Experimental)

Chapter Contents

Chapter 1
The CLP Procedure (Experimental)

Overview

The CLP procedure is a finite domain constraint programming solver for constraint satisfaction problems (CSPs) with linear, logical, global, and scheduling constraints. In addition to having an expressive syntax for representing CSPs, the solver features powerful built-in consistency routines and constraint propagation algorithms, a choice of nondeterministic search strategies, and controls for guiding the search mechanism that enable you to solve a diverse array of combinatorial problems.

For the most recent updates to the documentation for this experimental procedure, see the Statistics and Operations Research Documentation page at http://support.sas.com/rnd/app/doc.html.

The Constraint Satisfaction Problem

Many important problems in areas such as Artificial Intelligence (AI) and Operations Research (OR) can be formulated as constraint satisfaction problems. A CSP is defined by a finite set of variables taking values from finite domains and a finite set of constraints restricting the values the variables can simultaneously take.

More formally, a CSP can be defined as a triple $\langle X, D, C \rangle$ where

- $X = \{x_1, \ldots, x_n\}$ is a finite set of *variables*.
- $D = \{D_1, \ldots, D_n\}$ is a finite set of *domains*, where D_i is a finite set of possible values that the variable x_i can take. D_i is known as the *domain* of variable x_i.
- $C = \{c_1, \ldots, c_m\}$ is a finite set of *constraints* restricting the values that the variables can simultaneously take.

Note that the domains need not represent consecutive integers. For example, the domain of a variable could be the set of all *even* numbers in the interval [0, 100]. A domain does not even need to be totally numeric. In fact, in a scheduling problem with resources, the values are typically multidimensional. For example, an activity can be considered as a variable and each element of the domain would be an *n-tuple* that represents a start time for the activity as well as the resource(s) that must be assigned to the activity corresponding to the start time.

A solution to a CSP is an assignment of values to the variables in order to satisfy all the constraints, and the problem amounts to finding solution(s), or possibly determining that a solution does not exist.

The CLP procedure can be used to find one or more (and in some instances, all) solutions to a CSP with linear, logical, global, and scheduling constraints. The numeric components of all variable domains are assumed to be integers.

Techniques for Solving CSPs

Several techniques for solving CSPs are available. Kumar (1992) and Tsang (1993) present a good overview of these techniques.

It should be noted that the Satisfiability problem (SAT) (Garey and Johnson 1979) can be regarded as a CSP. Consequently, most problems in this class are NP-complete problems, and a backtracking search is an important technique for solving them (Floyd 1967). However, a backtracking approach is not very efficient due to the late detection of conflicts; that is, it is oriented toward *recovering* from failures and not *avoiding* them to begin with. The search space is reduced only after detection of a failure, and the performance of this technique drastically reduces with increasing problem size.

Constraint Propagation

A more efficient technique is that of constraint propagation, which uses consistency techniques to effectively prune the domains of variables. Consistency techniques are also known as relaxation algorithms (Tsang 1993) and the process is also referred to as problem reduction, domain filtering, or pruning. The research on consistency techniques originated with the Waltz filtering algorithm (Waltz 1975). Constraint propagation is characterized by the extent of propagation (also referred to as the level of consistency) and the domain pruning scheme that is followed — domain propagation or interval propagation. In practice, interval propagation is preferred over domain propagation due to its lower computational costs. This mechanism is discussed in detail in Van Hentenryck (1989). However, constraint propagation is not a complete solution technique and needs to be complemented by a search technique to ensure success (Kumar 1992).

Finite Domain Constraint Programming

Finite domain constraint programming is an effective and complete solution technique that embeds incomplete constraint propagation techniques into a nondeterministic backtracking search mechanism, implemented as follows. Whenever a node is visited, constraint propagation is carried out to attain a desired level of consistency. If the domain of each variable reduces to a singleton set, the node represents a solution to the CSP. If the domain of a variable becomes empty, the node is pruned. Otherwise a variable is selected, its domain distributed, and a new set of CSPs generated, each of which is a child node of the current node. Several factors play a role in determining the outcome of this mechanism, such as the extent of propagation (or level of consistency enforced), the variable selection strategy, and the variable assignment or domain distribution strategy.

For example, the lack of any propagation reduces this technique to a simple generate and test, whereas performing consistency on variables already selected reduces this to chronological backtracking, one of the systematic search techniques. These are also known as look-back schemas as they share the disadvantage of late conflict detection. Look-ahead schemas, on the other hand, work to prevent future conflicts. Some popular examples of look-ahead strategies in increasing degree of consistency level are Forward Checking (FC), Partial Look Ahead (PLA), and Full Look Ahead (LA) (Kumar 1992). Forward Checking enforces consistency between the current variable and future variables; PLA and LA extend this even further to pairs of not yet instantiated variables.

Two important consequences of this technique are that inconsistencies are discovered early on and that the current set of alternatives coherent with the existing partial solution is dynamically maintained. These consequences are powerful enough to prune large parts of the search tree, thereby reducing the "combinatorial explosion" of the search process. However, although constraint propagation at each node results in fewer nodes in the search tree, the processing at each node is more expensive. The ideal scenario is to strike a balance between the extent of propagation and the subsequent computation cost.

Variable selection is another strategy that can affect the solution process. The order in which variables are chosen for instantiation can have substantial impact on the complexity of the backtrack search. Several heuristics have been developed and analyzed for selecting variable ordering. One of the more common ones is a dynamic heuristic based on the *fail first* principle (Haralick and Elliot 1980), which selects the variable whose domain has minimal size. Subsequent analysis of this heuristic by several researchers has validated this technique as providing substantial improvement for a significant class of problems. Another popular technique is to instantiate the most constrained variable first. Both these strategies are based on the principle of selecting the variable most likely to fail and to detect such failures as early as possible.

The domain distribution strategy for a selected variable is yet another area that can influence the performance of a backtracking search. However, good value ordering heuristics are expected to be very problem-specific (Kumar 1992).

The CLP Procedure

The CLP procedure is a finite domain constraint programming solver for CSPs. In the context of the CLP procedure, CSPs can be classified into two types: standard CSPs and scheduling CSPs. A standard CSP is characterized by integer variables, linear constraints, array type constraints, global constraints, and reified constraints. In other words, X is a finite set of integer variables, and C can contain linear, array, global, or logical constraints. A scheduling CSP is characterized by activities, temporal constraints, and resource requirement constraints. In other words, X is a finite set of activities, and C is a set of temporal constraints and resource requirement constraints. The CSP type is indicated by specifying either the OUT= option or the SCHEDDATA= option in the PROC CLP statement.

Specification of the OUT= option in the PROC CLP statement indicates to the CLP procedure that the CSP is a standard type. As such, the procedure will expect VAR, LINCON, REIFY, ALLDIFF, ARRAY, and FOREACH statements. You can also specify a Problem data set using the DATA= option in the PROC CLP statement in lieu of, or in combination with, VAR and LINCON statements.

Specification of the SCHEDDATA= option in the PROC CLP statement indicates to the CLP procedure that the CSP is a scheduling type. As such, the procedure will expect ACTIVITY, RESOURCE, REQUIRES, and SCHEDULE statements. You can also specify an Activity data set using the ACTDATA= option in the PROC CLP statement in lieu of, or in combination with, the ACTIVITY and LINCON statements. Precedence relationships between activities must be defined using the ACTDATA= data set. Resource requirements of activities must be defined using the RESOURCE and REQUIRES statements.

The output data set contains any solutions determined by the CLP procedure. For more information on the format and layout, see the "Details" section on page 24.

Consistency Techniques

The CLP procedure features a Full Look-Ahead algorithm for standard CSPs that follows a strategy of maintaining a version of Generalized Arc Consistency that is based on the AC-3 Consistency routine (Mackworth 1977). This strategy maintains consistency between the selected variable and the unassigned variables and also maintains consistency between unassigned variables. For the scheduling CSPs, the CLP procedure uses a Forward Checking algorithm, an arc-consistency routine for maintaining consistency between unassigned activities, and energetic-based reasoning methods for resource-constrained scheduling that feature the Edge Finder algorithm (Applegate and Cook 1991). You can elect to turn off some of these consistency techniques in the interest of performance.

Selection Strategy

A search algorithm for CSPs searches systematically through the possible assignments of values to variables. The order in which a variable is selected can be based on a *static* ordering, which is determined before the search begins, or on a *dynamic* ordering, in which the choice of the next variable depends on the current state of the search. The VARSELECT= option in the PROC CLP statement defines the variable selection strategy for a standard CSP. The default strategy is the dynamic MINR strategy, which selects the variable with the smallest range. The ACTSELECT= option in the SCHEDULE statement defines the activity selection strategy for a scheduling CSP. The default strategy is the RAND strategy, which selects an activity at random from the set of activities that begin prior to the earliest early finish time. This strategy was proposed by Nuijten (1994).

Assignment Strategy

Once a variable or an activity has been selected, the assignment strategy dictates the value that is assigned to it. For variables, the assignment strategy is specified with the VARASSIGN= option in the PROC CLP statement. The default assignment strategy selects the minimum value from the domain of the selected variable. For activities, the assignment strategy is specified with the ACTASSIGN= option in the SCHEDULE statement. The default strategy of RAND assigns the time to the earliest start time, and the resources are chosen randomly from the set of resource assignments that support the selected start time.

Introductory Examples

The following examples illustrate the formulation and solution of two well-known logical puzzles in the constraint programming community using the CLP procedure.

Send More Money

The Send More Money problem consists of finding unique digits for the letters D, E, M, N, O, R, S, and Y such that S and M are different from zero (no leading zeros) and the equation

$$SEND + MORE = MONEY$$

is satisfied. The unique solution of the problem is $9567 + 1085 = 10652$.

Using PROC CLP, we can solve this problem as follows:

```
proc clp dom=[0,9]              /* Define the default domain */
    out=out;                    /* Name the output data set  */
   var S E N D M O R E M O N E Y;/* Declare the variables     */
   lincon                       /* Linear constraints        */
                                /* SEND + MORE = MONEY        */
      1000*S + 100*E + 10*N + D + 1000*M + 100*O + 10*R + E
      =
      10000*M + 1000*O + 100*N  + 10*E + Y,
      S<>0,                     /* No leading zeros           */
      M<>0;
   alldiff();   /* All variables have pairwise distinct values*/
   run;
```

Obs	S	E	N	D	M	O	R	Y
1	9	5	6	7	1	0	8	2

Figure 1.1. Solution to SEND + MORE = MONEY

Eight Queens

The Eight Queens problem is a special instance of the N-Queens problem where the objective is to position N queens on an $N \times N$ chessboard such that no two queens attack each other. The CLP procedure provides an expressive constraint for variable arrays that can be used for solving this problem very efficiently.

Since each queen must occupy a distinct row, we can model this using a variable array A of dimension N, where $A[i]$ is the row number of the queen in column i. Since no two queens can be on the same row, it follows that all the $A[i]$'s must be pairwise distinct.

In order to ensure that no two queens can be on the same diagonal, we must have the following for all i and j:

$$A[j] - A[i] <> j - i$$

and

$$A[j] - A[i] <> i - j$$

In other words,

$$A[i] - i <> A[j] - j$$

and

$$A[i] + i <> A[j] + j$$

Hence, the $(A[i] + i)$'s are pairwise distinct, and the $(A[i] - i)$'s are pairwise distinct. The CLP procedure can be used to find a solution to this problem, as follows:

```
proc clp out=out
        varselect=fifo; /* Variable Selection Strategy           */
    array A[8] (A1-A8);   /* Define the array A                  */
    var (A1-A8)=[1,8];    /* Define each of the variables in the array */
                          /* Initialize domains                  */
    /* A[i] is the row number of the queen in column i*/
    foreach(A, DIFF,  0); /* A[i] 's are pairwise distinct */
    foreach(A, DIFF, -1); /* A[i] - i 's are pairwise distinct */
    foreach(A, DIFF,  1); /* A[i] + i 's are pairwise distinct */
    run;
```

Obs	A1	A2	A3	A4	A5	A6	A7	A8
1	1	5	8	6	3	7	2	4

Figure 1.2.   A Solution to the Eight Queens Problem

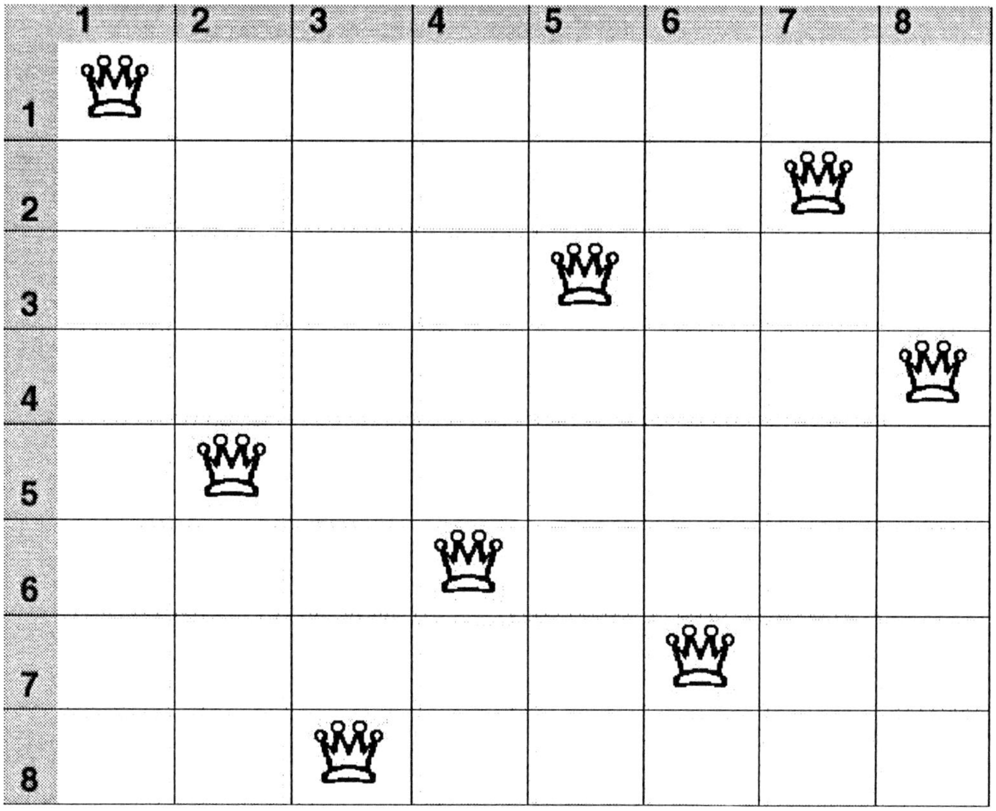

Figure 1.3. A Solution to the Eight Queens Problem

Syntax

The following statements are used in PROC CLP:

> **PROC CLP** *options* ;
>> **ACTIVITY** *activity specifications* ;
>> **ALLDIFF** *alldiff constraints* ;
>> **ARRAY** *array specifications* ;
>> **FOREACH** *foreach constraints* ;
>> **LINCON** *linear constraints* ;
>> **REIFY** *reified constraints* ;
>> **REQUIRES** *resource requirement constraints* ;
>> **RESOURCE** *resource specifications* ;
>> **SCHEDULE** *schedule options* ;
>> **VAR** *variable specifications* ;

Functional Summary

The following tables outline the options available for the CLP procedure classified by function.

Table 1.1. Assignment Strategy Options

Description	Statement	Option
activity assignment strategy	SCHEDULE	ACTASSIGN=
variable assignment strategy	PROC CLP	VARASSIGN=

Table 1.2. Data Set Options

Description	Statement	Option
activity input data set	PROC CLP	ACTDATA=
problem input data set	PROC CLP	DATA=
solution output data set	PROC CLP	OUT=
schedule output data set	PROC CLP	SCHEDDATA=

Table 1.3. General Options

Description	Statement	Option
suppress preprocessing	PROC CLP	NOPREPROCESS

Table 1.4. Output Control Options

Description	Statement	Option
find all possible solutions	PROC CLP	FINDALLSOLNS
indicate progress in log	PROC CLP	SHOWPROGRESS
number of solutions	PROC CLP	SOLNS=

Table 1.5. Scheduling CSP Statements

Description	Statement	Option
activity specifications	ACTIVITY	
resource requirement specifications	REQUIRES	
resource specifications	RESOURCE	
schedule options	SCHEDULE	

Table 1.6. Scheduling Temporal Constraints Options

Description	Statement	Option
activity duration	ACTIVITY	DURATION=
activity start lower bound	ACTIVITY	SGE=
activity start upper bound	ACTIVITY	SLE=
activity finish lower bound	ACTIVITY	FGE=
activity finish upper bound	ACTIVITY	FLE=
schedule duration	SCHEDULE	DURATION=
schedule start	SCHEDULE	START=
schedule finish	SCHEDULE	FINISH=

Table 1.7. Scheduling Search Control Options

Description	Statement	Option
deadend multiplier	PROC CLP	DEM=
number of allowable deadends per restart	PROC CLP	DEPR=
number of search restarts	PROC CLP	RESTARTS=
edge finder consistency routine	SCHEDULE	EF

Table 1.8. Selection Strategy Options

Description	Statement	Option
activity selection strategy	SCHEDULE	ACTSELECT=
variable selection strategy	PROC CLP	VARSELECT=

Table 1.9. Standard CSP Statements

Description	Statement	Option
alldifferent constraints	ALLDIFF	
array specifications	ARRAY	
foreach constraints	FOREACH	
linear constraints	LINCON	
reified constraints	REIFY	
variable specifications	VAR	

PROC CLP Statement

PROC CLP *options* ;

The following options can appear in the PROC CLP statement.

ACTDATA=*SAS-data-set*
ACTIVITY=*SAS-data-set*

identifies the input data set that defines the activities and temporal constraints. The temporal constraints consist of time alignment type constraints and precedence type constraints. The format of the ACTDATA= data set is similar to the Activity data set used by the CPM procedure in SAS/OR software. The activities and time alignment constraints can also be directly specified using the ACTIVITY statement without the need for a data set. The CLP procedure enables you to define activities using a combination of the two specifications.

DATA=*SAS-data-set*

identifies the input data set that defines the linear constraints. The format of the DATA= data set is similar to that used by the LP procedure in SAS/OR software. The linear constraints can also be specified inline using the LINCON statement. The CLP procedure enables you to define linear constraints using a combination of the two specifications. When defining linear constraints, you must define the structural variables using a VAR statement.

DEM=*d*

specifies the deadend multiplier for the CSP. The deadend multiplier is used to determine the number of deadends that are permitted before triggering a complete restart of the search technique in a scheduling environment. The number of deadends is the product of the deadend multiplier and the number of unassigned activities. The default value is 0.15. This option is valid only with the SCHEDDATA= option.

DEPR=*n*

specifies the number of deadends that are permitted before PROC CLP restarts or terminates the search, depending on whether or not a randomized search strategy is used. In the case of a nonrandomized strategy, *n* is an upper bound on the number of allowable deadends before terminating. In the case of a randomized strategy, *n* is an upper bound on the number of allowable deadends before restarting the search. The DEPR= option has priority over the DEM= option. The default value of the DEPR= option is ∞.

DOMAIN=[*lb, ub***]**
DOM=[*lb, ub***]**

specifies the global domain of all variables to be the closed interval [*lb, ub*]. You can override the global domain for a variable with a VAR statement or the DATA= data set.

FINDALLSOLNS
ALLSOLNS
FAS
FINDALL

attempts to find all possible solutions to the CSP. When a randomized search strategy is used, it is possible to rediscover the same solution and end up with multiple instances of the same solution. This is currently the case when solving scheduling-related problems. Therefore, this option is ignored when solving a scheduling-related problem.

NOPREPROCESS

suppresses any preprocessing that would typically be performed for the problem.

OUT=*SAS-data-set*

identifies the output data set that contains the solution(s) to the CSP, if any exist. Each observation in the OUT= data set corresponds to a solution of the CSP. The number of solutions generated can be controlled using the SOLNS= option in the PROC CLP statement.

RESTARTS=*n*

specifies the number of restarts of the randomized search technique before terminating the procedure. The default value is 3.

SCHEDDATA=*SAS-data-set*
SCHEDULE=*SAS-data-set*

identifies the output data set that contains the scheduling-related solution to the CSP, if one exists. Each observation in the SCHEDDATA= data set corresponds to an activity. The format of the schedule data set is similar to the schedule data set generated by the CPM and PM procedures in SAS/OR software. The number of solutions generated can be controlled using the SOLNS= option in the PROC CLP statement.

SHOWPROGRESS

prints a message to the log whenever a solution has been found. When a randomized strategy is used, the number of restarts and deadends that were required are also printed to the log.

SOLNS=*n*

specifies the number of solution attempts to be generated for the CSP. The default value is 1. It is important to note, especially in the context of randomized strategies, that an attempt could result in no solution, given the current controls on the search mechanism, such as the number of restarts and the number of deadends permitted. As a result, the total number of solutions found may not match the SOLNS= parameter.

VARASSIGN=*keyword*
VALSELECT=*keyword*

specifies the value selection strategy. Currently there is only one value selection strategy. The MIN strategy selects the minimum value from the domain of the selected variable. To assign activities, use the ACTASSIGN= option in the SCHEDULE statement.

VARSELECT=*keyword*

specifies the variable selection strategy. Both static and dynamic strategies are available. Possible values are as follows.

Static strategies:

- FIFO: Uses the First-In-First-Out ordering of the variables as encountered by the procedure.
- MAXCS: Selects the variable with the maximum number of constraints.

Dynamic strategies:

- MINR: Selects the variable with the smallest range (that is, the minimum value of upper bound minus lower bound).
- MAXC: Selects the variable with the largest number of active constraints.
- MINRMAXC: Selects the variable with the smallest range, breaking ties by selecting the one with the largest number of active constraints.

The dynamic strategies embody the "Fail First Principle" (FFP) of Haralick and Elliot (1980), which suggests that "To succeed, try first where you are most likely to fail." The default strategy is MINR. To select activities, use the ACTSELECT= option in the SCHEDULE statement.

ACTIVITY Statement

ACTIVITY *activity* < = (< DUR= > *dur* [*altype*=*aldate* ...]) > ;
ACTIVITY *(activity_list)* < = (< DUR= > *dur* [*altype*=*aldate* ...]) > ;

where *dur* is the activity duration and *altype* is a keyword specifying an alignment type constraint on the activity (or activities) with respect to the date given by *aldate*.

The ACTIVITY statement defines one or more activities and the attributes of each activity, such as the duration and any temporal constraints of the time alignment type. The default duration is 1.

Valid values for the *altype* keyword are as follows:

- SGE: Start greater than or equal to *aldate*
- SLE: Start less than or equal to *aldate*
- FGE: Finish greater than or equal to *aldate*
- FLE: Finish less than or equal to *aldate*

You can specify any combination of the above keywords. For example, to define an activity A with duration 3 and to set the start time of activity A equal to 10, you would specify the following:

```
activity A = ( dur=3 sge=10 sle=10 );
```

You can alternatively use the ACTDATA= data set to define the activities, durations, and temporal constraints. In fact, you can specify both an ACTIVITY statement and an ACTDATA= data set. You must use an ACTDATA= data set to define precedence-related temporal constraints. The SCHEDDATA= option must be specified when the ACTIVITY statement is used.

ALLDIFF Statement

ALLDIFF *(variables)* ... ;
ALLDIFFERENT *(variables)* ... ;

The ALLDIFF statement can have multiple specifications. Each specification defines a unique global constraint on a set of variables requiring all of them to be different from each other. A global constraint is equivalent to a conjunction of elementary constraints.

For example, the statements

```
var (X1-X3) A B;
alldiff (X1-X3) (A B);
```

are equivalent to

$$X1 \neq X2$$
$$X2 \neq X3$$
$$X1 \neq X3$$
$$A \neq B$$

ARRAY Statement

ARRAY *arrayspec [, arrayspec...]*;

where *arrayspec := arrayname [dimensions] (variables)*;

The ARRAY statement is used to associate a name with a list of variables. Each of the variables in the variable list must be defined using a VAR statement. The ARRAY statement is required when specifying a FOREACH type constraint.

FOREACH Statement

FOREACH *(array, type, <offset <, constant > >)* ;

where *array* must be defined using an ARRAY statement, *type* is a keyword that determines the type of the constraint, and *offset* and *constant* are integers.

The FOREACH statement iteratively applies a constraint over an array of variables. The type of the constraint is determined by *type*. The optional *offset* and *constant* parameters are integers and are interpreted in the context of the constraint type.

Currently, the only valid value for *type* is DIFF.

The FOREACH statement corresponding to the DIFF keyword iteratively applies the following constraint to each pair of variables in the array:

$$A[i] + \textit{offset} \times i \; \neq \; A[j] + \textit{offset} \times j \quad \forall \, i \neq j, \; i,j = 1,\ldots,m$$

For example, the constraint that all $(A[i] - i)$'s are pairwise distinct for an array A is expressed as

```
foreach (A, diff, -1);
```

LINCON Statement

LINCON *l_con [, l_con ...]*;
LINEAR *l_con [, l_con ...]*;

where *l_con := linear_term operator linear_term*

linear_term is of the following form:

$$((< + | - > \textit{variable} | \textit{number} < *\textit{variable} >)\ldots)$$

operator can be one of the following:

$$\leq, <, =, ==, \geq, >, <>, LE, EQ, GE, LT, GT, NE$$

The LINCON statement allows for a very general specification of linear constraints. In particular, it allows for specification of the following types of equality or inequality constraints:

$$\sum_{j=1}^{n} a_{ij}x_j \; \{\leq \mid < \mid = \mid \geq \mid > \mid \neq\} \; b_i \quad \text{for } i = 1, \ldots, m$$

For example, the constraint $4x_1 - 3x_2 = 5$ is expressed as

```
var x1 x2;
lincon 4 * x1 - 3 * x2 = 5;
```

and the constraints

$$10x_1 - x_2 \geq 10$$

$$x_1 + 5x_2 \neq 15$$

are expressed as

```
var x1 x2;
lincon 10 <= 10 * x1 - x2,
       x1 + 5 * x2 <> 15;
```

Note that variables can be specified on either side of an equality or inequality in a LINCON statement. Linear constraints can also be specified using the DATA= data set. When using a LINCON statement, you must define the variables using a VAR statement.

REIFY Statement

REIFY *variable : (l_con)...;*

where *l_con := linear_term operator linear_term*

linear_term is of the following form:

$$((< +|- > variable|number < *variable >)\ldots)$$

operator can be one of the following:

$$\leq, <, =, ==, \geq, >, <>, \text{LE}, \text{EQ}, \text{GE}, \text{LT}, \text{GT}, \text{NE}$$

The REIFY statement associates a binary variable with a linear constraint. The value of the binary variable is 1 or 0 depending on whether the linear constraint is satisfied or not, respectively. The linear constraint has been reified, and the logical variable is referred to as the control variable. As with the other variables, the control variable must also be defined in a VAR statement or in the DATA= data set.

The REIFY statement provides a convenient mechanism for expressing logical constraints, such as disjunctive and implicative constraints. For example, the disjunctive constraint

$$(3x + 4y < 20) \vee (5x - 2y > 50)$$

can be expressed with the following statements:

```
var x y p q;
reify p: (3 * x + 4 * y > 20) q: (5 * x - 2 * y) > 50);
lincon p + q >= 1;
```

The REIFY constraint can also be used to express a constraint involving the absolute value of a variable. For example, the constraint

$$|X| = 5$$

can be expressed with the following statements:

```
var x p q;
reify p: (x = 5) q: (x = -5);
lincon p + q = 1;
```

REQUIRES Statement

REQUIRES *activity_spec = (assignment_spec [, assignment_set_spec ...]);*
REQ *activity_spec = (assignment_spec [, assignment_set_spec ...]);*

where *activity_spec:= activity* or *(activity_list)*
and *assignment_spec:= resource* or *(resource_list)*

The REQUIRES statement defines the potential activity assignments with respect to the pool of resources. For example, the following statements specify that activity A requires resources R1 and R2 simultaneously *or* resources R3 and R4 simultaneously.

```
activity A;
resource R1-R4;
requires A= ((R1 R2), (R3 R4));
```

RESOURCE Statement

RESOURCE *(resource_spec) ...;*
RES *(resource_spec) ...;*

where *resource_spec* is *resource* or *(resource list)*

The RESOURCE statement specifies the names of all resources that are available to be allocated to the activities. The REQUIRES statement is necessary to specify the resource requirements of an activity. Currently all resources are assumed to be unary resources in that their capacity is equal to 1 and they may not be assigned to more than one activity at any given time.

SCHEDULE Statement

SCHEDULE *options*;

The following options can appear in the SCHEDULE statement.

ACTASSIGN=keyword
ACTVALSELECT=keyword

specifies the activity assignment strategy. The possible activity assignment strategies are as follows:

- RAND: Assign the activity to start at its earliest possible start time. If the activity has any resource requirements, then randomly select a resource requirement from the set of resource requirements that support the selected start time for the activity. Assign the activity to the resources specified in this requirement.

- MAXLS: Assign the activity to start at its earliest possible start time. If the activity has any resource requirements, then select the resource requirement with the latest start time from the set of resource requirements that support the selected start time for the activity. Assign the activity to the resources specified in this requirement.

The default strategy is RAND. For assigning variables, use the VARASSIGN= option in the PROC CLP statement.

ACTSELECT=keyword

specifies the activity selection strategy. The activity selection strategy can be randomized or deterministic, as described below.

The following are randomized selection strategies:

- RAND: Selects an activity at random from the set of activities that begin prior to the earliest early finish time. This strategy was proposed by Nuijten (1994).

- MINA: Selects an activity at random from the subset of activities that begin prior to the earliest early finish time that have the minimum number of resource assignments.

- MAXD: Selects an activity at random from the subset of activities that begin prior to the earliest early finish time that have maximum duration.

- MINLS: Selects an activity at random from the subset of activities that begin prior to the earliest early finish time that have a minimum late start date.

The following are deterministic selection strategies:

- DET: Selects the first activity that begins prior to the earliest activity finish date.

- DMINLS: Selects the activity with the earliest late start time.

The default strategy is RAND. For selecting variables, use the VARSELECT= option in the PROC CLP statement.

DURATION=*dur*
SCHEDDUR=*dur*
DUR=*dur*

specifies the duration of the schedule. The DURATION= option imposes a constraint that the duration of the schedule does not exceed the specified value.

EF
EDGEFINDER

activates the edge finder consistency routines for scheduling problems. By default, the EF option is inactive.

FINISH=*finish*
END=*finish*
FINISHBEFORE=*finish*

specifies the finish time for the schedule. The schedule finish time is an upper bound on the finish time of each activity (subject to time, precedence, and resource constraints). If you wish to impose a tighter upper bound for an activity, you can do so either by using the FLE= option in an ACTIVITY statement or by using the _ALIGNDATE_ and _ALIGNTYPE_ variables in the ACTDATA= data set.

START=*start*
BEGIN=*start*
STARTAFTER=*start*

specifies the start time for the schedule. The schedule start time is a lower bound on the start time of each activity (subject to time, precedence, and resource constraints). If you wish to impose a tighter lower bound for an activity, you can do so either by using the SGE= option in an ACTIVITY statement or by using the _ALIGNDATE_ and _ALIGNTYPE_ variables in the ACTDATA= data set.

VAR Statement

VAR STATEMENT *varspec [,varspec ...]*;

where *varspec := variable <=<lb <,ub>>;*
or *varspec := (variable list) <=<lb <,ub>>;*

The VAR statement specifies all the variables and their domains that are to be considered in the CSP. Any variable domains specified in a VAR statement override the default variable domains. If *lb* is specified and *ub* is omitted, the corresponding variable(s) are considered as being assigned to *lb*.

Details

This section provides a detailed outline of the use of the CLP procedure. The material is organized in subsections that describe different aspects of the procedure.

Modes of Operation

The CLP procedure can be invoked in one of two modes: standard mode and scheduling mode. The standard mode gives you access to linear constraints, reified constraints, alldiff constraints, and array constraints, whereas the scheduling mode gives you access to more scheduling-specific constraints such as temporal constraints (precedence and time) and resource constraints. In standard mode, the decision variables are one-dimensional; a variable is assigned an integer in a solution. In scheduling mode, the variables are typically multidimensional; a variable is assigned a start time and possibly a set of resources in a solution. In scheduling mode, the variables are referred to as activities and the solution is referred to as a schedule.

Selecting the Mode of Operation

The CLP procedure requires the specification of an output data set to store the solution(s) to the CSP. There are two possible output data sets: the Solution data set (specified using the OUT= option in the PROC CLP statement), which corresponds to the standard mode of operation, and the Schedule data set (specified using the SCHEDDATA= option in the PROC CLP statement), which corresponds to the scheduling mode of operation. The mode is determined by which output data set has been specified. If an output data set is not specified, the procedure terminates with an error message. If both output data sets have been specified, the Schedule data set is ignored.

Activity Data Set

You can use an Activity data set in lieu of, or in combination with, an ACTIVITY statement to define activities and constraints relating to the activities. The Activity data set is similar to the Activity data set input to the CPM procedure in SAS/OR software and is specified using the ACTDATA= option in the PROC CLP statement.

The Activity data set enables you to define an activity, its domain, and any temporal constraints. The temporal constraints could be either time alignment type or precedence type constraints. The Activity data set requires, at the minimum, two variables: one to determine the activity, and another to determine its duration. The procedure terminates if it cannot find the required variables. The activity is determined with the _ACTIVITY_ variable, and the duration is determined with the _DURATION_ variable. In addition to the mandatory variables, you can also specify temporal constraints related to the activities.

Time Alignment Constraints

The _ALIGNDATE_ and _ALIGNTYPE_ variables enable you to define time alignment type constraints. The _ALIGNTYPE_ variable defines the type of the alignment constraint for the activity named in the _ACTIVITY_ variable with respect to the _ALIGNDATE_ variable. If the _ALIGNDATE_ variable is not present in the Activity data set, the _ALIGNTYPE_ variable is ignored. If the _ALIGNDATE_ is present but the _ALIGNTYPE_ variable is missing, the alignment type is assumed to be SGE. The _ALIGNTYPE_ variable can take the values shown in Table 1.10:

Table 1.10. Valid Values for the _ALIGNTYPE_ Variable

Value	Type of Alignment
SEQ	Start equal to
SGE	Start greater than or equal to
SLE	Start less than or equal to
FEQ	Finish equal to
FGE	Finish greater than or equal to
FLE	Finish less than or equal to

Precedence Constraints

The _SUCCESSOR_ variable enables you to define precedence type relationships between activities using AON (Activity-On-Node) format. The _SUCCESSOR_ variable must have the same type as that of the _ACTIVITY_ variable. The _LAG_ variable defines the lag type of the relationship. By default, all precedence relationships are considered to be *Finish-to-Start (FS)*. An FS type of precedence relationship is also referred to as a *standard* precedence constraint. All other types of precedence relationships are considered to be nonstandard precedence constraints. The _LAGDUR_ variable specifies the lag duration. By default, the lag duration is zero.

For each (activity, successor) pair, you can define a lag type and a lag duration. Consider the pair of activities (A, B) with a lag duration given by *lagdur*. The interpretation of each of the different lag types is given in Table 1.11.

Table 1.11. Valid Values for the _LAG_ Variable

Lag Type	Interpretation
FS	Finish A + lagdur $\leq$ Start B
SS	Start A + lagdur $\leq$ Start B
FF	Finish A + lagdur $\leq$ Finish B
SF	Start A + lagdur $\leq$ Finish B
FSE	Finish A + lagdur = Start B
SSE	Start A + lagdur = Start B
FFE	Finish A + lagdur = Finish B
SFE	Start A + lagdur = Finish B

The first four lag types (FS, SS, FF, and SF) are also referred to as *Finish-to-Start, Start-to-Start, Finish-to-Finish,* and *Start-to-Finish,* respectively. The next four types (FSE, SSE, FFE, and SFE) are stricter versions of FS, SS, FF, and SF, respectively. The first four types impose a lower bound on the start/finish times of B, while the last four types force the start/finish times to be set equal to the lower bound of the domain. This enables you to force an activity to begin when its predecessor is finished. It is relatively easy to generate infeasible scenarios with the stricter versions, so you should only use the stricter versions if the weaker versions are not adequate for your problem.

Resource Constraints

The Activity data set cannot be used to define resource requirement type constraints. To define resource requirement type constraints, you must specify RESOURCE and REQUIRES statements.

Variables in the ACTDATA= data set

Table 1.12 lists all the variables associated with the Activity data set and their interpretations by the CLP procedure. The table also lists for each variable its type (C for character, N for numeric), the possible values it can assume, and its default value.

Table 1.12. Activity Data Set Variables

Name	Type	Description	Allowed Values	Default
ACTIVITY	C/N	activity name		
DURATION	N	duration		0
SUCCESSOR	C/N	successor name	same type as _ACTIVITY_	
ALIGNDATE	N	alignment date		0
ALIGNTYPE	C	alignment type	SGE, SLE, SEQ, FGE, FLE, FEQ	SGE
LAG	C	lag type	FS, SS, FF, SF, FSE, SSE, FFE, SFE	FS
LAGDUR	N	lag duration		0

Schedule Data Set

In order to solve a scheduling type CSP, you need to specify a Schedule data set using the SCHEDDATA= option in the PROC CLP statement. The Schedule data set contains all the solutions that have been determined by the CLP procedure.

The Schedule data set always contains the following five variables: SOLUTION, ACTIVITY, DUR, START, and FINISH. If any resources have been specified, then there is also a variable corresponding to each resource with the name of the variable being the name of the resource. The SOLUTION variable gives the solution number that each observation corresponds to. The ACTIVITY variable identifies the activity, the DUR variable gives the duration of the activity, and the START and FINISH variables give the scheduled start and finish times for the activity. If there are resources present, the corresponding resource variable indicates whether or not it is being utilized for the activity.

For every solution found and for each activity, the Schedule data set contains an observation that lists the assignment information for that activity.

If an Activity data set has been specified, then the formats and labels for the ACTIVITY and DUR variables carry over to the Schedule data set.

Constraint Data Set

The Constraint data set defines linear constraints, variable types, and bounds on variable domains. You can use a Constraint data set in lieu of, or in combination with, a LINCON and/or a VAR statement in order to define linear constraints, variable types, and variable bounds. The Constraint data set is similar to the problem data set input to the LP procedure in SAS/OR software and is specified using the DATA= option in the PROC CLP statement.

The Constraint data set must be in dense input format. In the dense input format, a model's columns appear as variables in the input data set and the data set must contain the _TYPE_ variable, the _RHS_ variable, and at least one numeric variable. In the absence of the above requirement, the CLP procedure terminates. The _TYPE_ variable is a character variable which tells the CLP procedure how to interpret each observation. The CLP procedure recognizes the following keywords as valid values for the _TYPE_ variable: EQ, LE, GE, NE, LT, GT, LOWERBD, UPPERBD, BINARY, and FIXED. An optional character variable, _ID_, can be used to name each row in the Constraint data set.

Linear Constraints

For the _TYPE_ values EQ, LE, GE, NE, LT, GT, the corresponding observation is interpreted as a linear constraint. The _RHS_ variable is a numeric variable that contains the right-hand-side coefficient of the linear constraint. Any numeric variable other than _RHS_ is interpreted as a structural variable for the linear constraint.

Domain Bounds

The values LOWERBD and UPPERBD specify additional lower bounds and upper bounds on the variable domains. In an observation where the _TYPE_ variable is equal to LOWERBD, a nonmissing value for a decision variable is considered a lower bound for that variable. Similarly, in an observation where the _TYPE_ variable is equal to UPPERBD, a nonmissing values for a decision variable is considered an upper bound for that variable. In both the above instances, it is important to note that any specified lower or upper bounds on a variable must be consistent with the existing domain of the variable, or the problem is deemed infeasible.

Variable Types

The keywords BINARY and FIXED are interpreted as specifying numeric types. If the value of _TYPE_ is BINARY for an observation, then any decision variable with a nonmissing entry for the observation is interpreted as being a binary variable with domain {0,1}. If the value of _TYPE_ is FIXED for an observation, then any decision variable with a nonmissing entry for the observation is interpreted as being assigned to that nonmissing value. In other words, if the value of the variable X is c in an observation for which _TYPE_ is FIXED, then the domain of X is considered to be the singleton $\{c\}$. It is important to note that the value c should belong to the domain of X, or the problem is deemed infeasible.

Any numeric variable other than _RHS_ is implicitly considered as appearing in a VAR statement and does not require a separate definition in a VAR statement. In the event that a numeric variable has previously been defined in a VAR statement, any bounds that are defined in the Constraint data set are considered in addition to bounds that may have been defined using the VAR statement.

Variables in the DATA= data set

Table 1.13 lists all the variables associated with the Constraint data set and their interpretations by the CLP procedure. The table also lists for each variable its type (C for character, N for numeric), the possible values it can assume, and its default value.

Table 1.13. Constraint Data Set Variables

Name	Type	Description	Allowed Values	Default
TYPE	C	observation type	EQ, LE, GE, NE, LT, GT, LOWERBD, UPPERBD, BINARY, FIXED	
RHS	N	right-hand-side coefficient		0
_ID_	C	observation name (optional)		
Any numeric variable other than _RHS_	N	structural variable		

Solution Data Set

In order to solve a standard (nonscheduling) type CSP, you need to specify a Solution data set using the OUT= option in the PROC CLP statement. The Solution data set contains all the solutions that have been determined by the CLP procedure.

The Solution data set contains as many decision variables as have been defined in the call to PROC CLP. Every observation in the Solution data set corresponds to a solution to the CSP. If a Problem data set has been specified, then any variable formats and variable labels from the Problem data set carry over to the Solution data set.

References

Applegate, D. and Cook, W. (1991), "A Computational Study of the Job Shop Scheduling Problem," *ORSA Journal on Computing*, 3, 149–156.

Colmerauer, A. (1990), "An Introduction to PROLOG III," *Communications of the ACM*, 33, 70–90.

Floyd, R. W. (1967), "Nondeterministic Algorithms," *Journal of the ACM*, 14, 636–644.

Garey, M. R. and Johnson, D. S. (1979), *Computers and Intractability: A Guide to the Theory of NP-Completeness*, New York: W. H. Freeman & Co.

Haralick, R. M. and Elliot, G. L. (1980), "Increasing Tree Search Efficiency for Constraint Satisfaction Problems," *Artificial Intelligence*, 14, 263–313.

Jaffar, J. and Lassez, J. (1987), "Constraint Logic Programming," *Conference Record of the 14th Annual ACM Symposium in Principles of Programming Languages*, Munich, 111–119.

Kumar, V. (1992), "Algorithms for Constraint-Satisfaction Problems: A Survey," *AI Magazine*, 13, 32–44.

Mackworth, A. K. (1977), "Consistency in Networks of Relations," *Artificial Intelligence*, 8, 99–118.

Nemhauser, G. L. and Wolsey, L. A. (1988), *Integer and Combinatorial Optimization*, New York: John Wiley.

Nuijten, W. (1994), *Time and Resource Constrained Scheduling*, Ph.D. thesis, Eindhoven Institute of Technology.

Smith, B. M., Brailsford, S. C., Hubbard, P. M., and Williams, H. P. (1996), "The Progressive Party Problem: Integer Linear Programming and Constraint Programming Compared," *Constraints*, 1, 119–138.

Tsang, E. (1993), *Foundations of Constraint Satisfaction*, London: Academic Press.

Van Hentenryck, P. (1989), *Constraint Satisfaction in Logic Programming*, Cambridge, MA: MIT Press.

Van Hentenryck, P., Deville, Y., and Teng, C. (1992), "A Generic Arc-Consistency Algorithm and its Specializations," *Artificial Intelligence*, 57, 291–321.

Waltz, D. L. (1975), "Understanding Line Drawings of Scenes with Shadows," in P. H. Winston, ed., "The Psychology of Computer Vision," 19–91, New York: McGraw-Hill.

Williams, H. P. and Wilson, J. M. (1998), "Connections Between Integer Linear Programming and Constraint Logic Programming – An Overview and Introduction to the Cluster of Articles," *INFORMS Journal of Computing*, 10, 261–264.

Subject Index

Syntax Index

Your Turn

If you have comments or suggestions about *SAS/OR® 9.1 User's Guide: Constraint Programming,* please send them to us on a photocopy of this page or send us electronic mail.

For comments about this book, please return the photocopy to

SAS Publishing
SAS Campus Drive
Cary, NC 27513
E-mail: **yourturn@sas.com**

For suggestions about the software, please return the photocopy to

SAS Institute Inc.
Technical Support Division
SAS Campus Drive
Cary, NC 27513
E-mail: **suggest@sas.com**

Printed in the United States
25797LVS00001B/1-2

9 781590 472583